In Defense of Animalhood

Riya Aarini

In Defense of Animalhood

Text copyright © 2023 by Riya Aarini

All rights reserved. No part of this book may be reproduced, distributed or transmitted in any form or by any means, including photocopying, recording, or other electronic or mechanical methods, without prior written permission of the publisher, except in the case of brief quotations embodied in critical articles and reviews.

This is a work of fiction. Names, characters, businesses, places, events, locales, and incidents are either the products of the author's imagination or used in a fictitious manner. Any resemblance to actual persons, living or dead, or actual events is purely coincidental.

ISBN: 978-1-956496-27-7 (Hardcover)

ISBN: 978-1-956496-23-9 (Paperback)

ISBN: 978-1-956496-24-6 (eBook)

Library of Congress Control Number: 2022923191

First published in Austin, Texas, USA

Visit www.riyapresents.com

To those who help protect wildlife by supporting efforts toward conservation, not captivity.

CONTENTS

On Zoo Polar Bears 1

On California Condors 4

On the Fat Seals Club 7

On Cow Belches 10

On Circus Tigers 12

On the Dancing Monkey 15

On Zoo Orangutans 19

On Ocelot Translocations 22

On Zoo Giraffes 25

On Elephant Conservation 27

On Bird Banding 30

On Wild-Animal Crossing Signs 33

On the Black-Naped Pheasant-Pigeon 36

On the Elephant Liquor Heist 39

On Lifelong Crow Grudges 42

On World Lemur Day 45

CONTENTS

On Miami's Wild Macaws   48

On Sea Turtles and Plastic Bags   52

On Chained Elephants   55

On the Captive Robin   58

On Seahorse Love   61

On Albatrosses and Plastics   64

On Trophy Hunting   67

On Captive Orcas   70

On Foxhunting   72

On Zonkeys and Zorses   75

On Experimental Lab Beagles   78

On Arizona's Wild Horses   82

On Mountain Gorillas and Ecotourism   85

ON ZOO POLAR BEARS

"Psst!" Under the darkness of nightfall, Leo whispered to get Pat's attention from across the polar bear enclosure.

Annoyingly roused from his rest, Pat lifted his head and grumbled, "What?"

"Did you see Betty the other day shaking her head nonstop like she'd lost it?"

Pat yawned. "Yes."

"And did you see Frank obsessively swimming figure eights in the concrete swimming pool like a polar bear on the verge of going bonkers?"

"Sure did," replied Pat.

"Conditions in our enclosure just don't cut it. We crave extreme heat and cold. We need to defend our territories against rivals. We require 150,000 square miles to move around. Nothing in this zoo replicates the daily stimulations we need to thrive," said Leo.

Bored and tired, Pat yawned yet again. "What's your point?"

"Well, it's miserable in here, right?"

"Yeah, so what's new?"

With shifty black polar bear pupils, Leo rubbed his paws together in excitement under the light of the moon. "I've hatched an escape plan. You in?"

Intrigued, Pat slowly sat up. "And how's that going to work? Once we escape the zoo, it's not exactly like we can blend in walking down the streets of the Bronx in the middle of July." Pat managed to keep his wits about him—an exceptionally rare skill for an animal held in captivity.

"We'll find a getaway car."

"What? You can't even drive."

Leo didn't hesitate to justify his plan. "Well, if humans are dumb enough to kidnap 1,700-pound polar bears from our Arctic dens and force us into mind-numbing captivity, it must not be that hard."

Pat considered Leo's plan for a minute.

"Come on! We were at the top of the food chain in the Arctic. Now, we've been reduced to eating a fortified commercial diet: dog kibble and thawed rabbits, for goodness' sake. Don't you miss the excitement of hunting ringed seals? Tell me you don't want to smell the delicious scent of seal on the Arctic ice 20 miles away. Just say you don't want the freedom to swim 60 miles in the cold blue ocean, and I'll shut up. Think about it, Pat, the life we could live again!"

And so, under the rays of moonlight, the polar bears continued to hatch their escape plan from the zoo.

ON CALIFORNIA CONDORS

"I was raised by a puppet. How 'bout you?" Sally asked Alice. The two California condors sat atop a mountainous peak enjoying the breeze and the sun as it leisurely dipped into the horizon.

Alice whipped her naked head around. "You too? I always figured something was off about Mom and Pop, but I couldn't quite put my feather on it."

"Yep, that's what they were, puppets parading as our parents, feeding us, stroking us, and just being there, pretending like nothing was awry," explained Sally. "Condor puppets raised us chicks to prevent us from becoming attached to the human puppeteers behind them."

"Ooh." Alice stared blankly out over the vast cavernous valley.

"Not only did they look ridiculous, but they were clumsy at feeding time. Thankfully, meat magically appeared in the incubator every day, but the puppet parents seemed to be all thumbs, barely able to skillfully push the food down our beaks, like a real bird would. We basically fed ourselves, picking the carrion from the stone bowl and gulping it down at almost every single meal," complained Sally.

"And their touch wasn't delicate in the least sense of the word."

"Mm-hmm. More like a blundering, uncoordinated bonk on the head than an affectionate caress." Sally stood briefly to ruffle her feathers, then sat down and continued gazing out from the top of the mountain.

Both condors sat in thoughtful silence.

Alice sighed. "It's no wonder we're socially inept, preferring to pick at garbage than socialize with other condors."

"But at least our numbers grew. When I was a chick, there were only 22 of us left flying around in the wild. We were such important birds," Sally boasted, "that the government put us at the top of the endangered species list and started a recovery program, complete with built-in puppet parents, to increase our population."

Feeling a whoosh of pride, Alice raised her head a little higher. "There are now over 300 of us socially awkward condors more excited to watch rock climbers ascend the side of the mountain than mingle with the rest of the flock."

The mountain wind blew.

Sally grunted. "I blame it all on the parenting."

"Meh, me too."

ON THE FAT SEALS CLUB

"Humph. I can't believe Charlemagne was kicked out of the Fat Seals Club," grumbled Stanley, a 7,000-pound seal swimming through the ocean.

"Yep, what a loss to the club. We need to be as blubbery as possible to insulate ourselves in the cold ocean water, store our energy, and stay buoyant," replied Griswold. "For seals like us, it's all about survival of the chunkiest."

"Yeah, being a slim seal is a death sentence."

"Getting kicked out wasn't his fault." Griswold paddled casually through the sea. "After all, despite his massive size and power, he couldn't prevent himself from being caught in a horrible ghost net."

"Abominable."

"The thick fishing net was 30 feet long, stretching longer than his 20-foot body." Griswold looked out vigilantly for sharks and killer whales as he swam. "Being as playful as he was, a quality he admirably kept through adulthood, Char explored an abandoned net fallen onto a coral reef. He stuck his curious nose into it, and *Bam!* He became horrendously trapped. With the net growing tighter and tighter around his neck and fins with every paddle, he could no longer hunt fish and squid. In no time, he lost an enormous amount of weight and became dangerously skinny."

"Since he failed to meet the weight requirement, he got kicked out of the Fat Seals Club. No more of the secret fin shake, no more feasting together on nine-course meals of scrumptious fish platters and squid soup, no more celebrations of corpulence for him. I missed him dearly at the monthly meetings," Stanley said wistfully. "I don't know why humans can't keep their 640,000 tons of fishing gear to themselves."

"Right, it takes months or years of storms and rough weather to break up the ghost nets discarded carelessly into the ocean," muttered Griswold.

"Don't the humans know better?"

Griswold lit up. "All fishermen have to do is return their unwanted fishing gear to the port for recycling instead of dumping it in the ocean, or implement a fishing gear buyback program or introduce biodegradable fishing nets that perform as well as nonbiodegradable ones. How hard can it be to convince them?"

Stanley shook his furry head in puzzlement. "Uh, fortunately for Char, a group of friendly surfers found him struggling under the ghost net and cut him free. Not all seals are so lucky; some die horrible deaths by drowning or slow starvation."

"Now that he's free from the entrapment of the ghost net, he's put his weight back on."

"I'm proud that good ol' Charlemagne has returned to a healthy 8,000 pounds and his membership to the Fat Seals Club has been reinstated." Stanley beamed.

"The bigger the better."

"Word."

ON COW BELCHES

Munching on cow cookies, Bessie chatted with Clarabelle in a grassy pasture. "So the humans have caught on," she said matter-of-factly.

Clarabelle casually lifted her head. "Huh?"

"They blame us for being among the biggest contributors to climate change."

"How so? We're practically harmless, silently grazing in the fields all day, maybe mooing every now and then, at the most. We selflessly give them milk, and they churn it into melt-in-your-mouth butter or curdle it into all sorts of fancy cheeses: aged Gouda, Camembert, and the wholesome cheddar, cut into chunks or melted into dip that's perfect with baked potato wedges. We provide humans with delicious feasts beyond measure. No cow has ever hurt a soul," replied Clarabelle, mindlessly chewing on her treat.

"Well, they figure our burps release 40 percent of methane emissions."

Clarabelle suddenly stopped chewing. "The greenhouse gas?" she asked wide-eyed.

"Yup, and it's all because we eat a high-fiber diet." Bessie silently gazed ahead, munching ever so slowly. The cows continued noshing on the cookies and grass. "Figures," Bessie finally blurted out, "humans will blame everything and everyone else for climate change—including grazing cows who mind our own business and have never hurt a fly, even the horn flies we swat with our tails but always miss."

Bessie and Clarabelle continued peacefully chewing, stopped to release loud, drawn-out burps, then looked at each other startled. "There you have it: the harbingers of the end of the world as we know it."

ON CIRCUS TIGERS

"Hey, so what's your story, Squiggly?" The young tiger pranced around light-footed in his four-foot-by-eight-foot cage, which stood next to a full-grown tiger's equally sized cage. Despite the cub's playfulness, the older tiger remained composed.

"*Hey?*" the adult tiger thundered. "My name is not Squiggly."

"Well, the ringleader calls you Squiggly."

"I don't care what the ringleader calls me. My name is Shiwen. And I don't have a story."

"Uh, not so. Everyone's got a story. My story is that one day I was play-fighting in the forests of Asia with my sister, Min. The next thing I knew, poachers ripped me from my family and, through the illegal wildlife trade, brought me to this circus act. Now they call me Stripes."

Unimpressed, the aged tiger turned his back to the cub, lay down, and looked out through the bars of his cage.

"What's his beef?" the inquisitive cub asked a tiger stuck in a cage on the opposite side.

"Don't mind proud Shiwen. He's getting old, beaten into submission for way too many years. He said the circus would never break him, but deep down I think it already has." The tiger paused, then said with spirit, "Nice to make your acquaintance. They call me Blue."

"And I'm Stripes, as you may have heard. I'm a little worried about Shiwen."

"We all should be. But the circus doesn't care. We're forced to put on a great show, but when the tent comes down, the horrible darkness takes over."

"How so? Obviously being new here, I wouldn't know," Stripes squealed with the innocence of a babe.

"Well, for one thing, when we're not performing in the circus, we spend almost all our time confined to these cages. It's nerve-racking. Wild tigers like us have the primitive need to hunt in territories that span 40 square miles. We stalk our prey, chase them for a good hour, and, if we're lucky, relish our meal. But in the circus landscape, we're denied the ability to follow our instinctual desires."

Stripes looked wide-eyed at his new friend.

"Without the enrichment from our natural forest habitat, some of us end up pacing frantically, as if that somehow makes up for our need to run, or bobbing our heads insanely, or being just plain miserable."

"Why do they do that to us?" Stripes asked.

"Uh, it's all done for the entertainment of humans," replied Blue.

"Oh." Stripes looked at his feet, unable to make sense of what he heard.

Blue lay down and relaxed as much as a captive circus tiger could in a cage. "Humph. I could never understand why they don't just turn on the TV and watch reruns of *The Beverly Hillbillies* for entertainment."

With the air of a king, Shiwen finally turned his head, and spoke. "I wonder the very same thing, Blue. It was the greatest show on earth."

ON THE DANCING MONKEY

A wild macaque from the world's third-largest tropical forest hopped into the bustling capital city on the island of Indonesia.

He spotted a chained macaque on the street and stopped out of curiosity. "We live in the midst of miles of gorgeous sandy beaches and a clear blue ocean that stretches forever. What are you doing chained up instead of enjoying the scenery?" he asked dumbfounded.

With furrowed brows and a grimace, the enslaved macaque thundered, "I've got news for you. It's not all afternoons of surfing and sunbathing for me. I'm forced to work for a living."

"Well," said the free macaque, scratching his head. "Are the wages impressive?"

"Impressive?" The chained macaque spat on the ground. "No matter how hard I work, I don't see a single rupiah from my constant efforts. I don't get to explore the colorful bazaars for a new red scarf or buy fried noodles from the street vendors selling everything from seasoned stir-fried rice to *bakso* meatball soup." The chained macaque looked down at the shackles on his feet. "Instead, I'm chained night and day, sometimes with my hands agonizingly clasped behind my back—except when I perform."

A two-seater sped by on the dusty, busy road. "Even when I'm zooming down the sidewalk on a mini motorcycle or teetering precariously on a unicycle at the edge of the street or walking on stilts with a fake smile plastered across my face, I'm wretchedly tethered to a metal chain that's impossible for a tiny macaque like me to break free from."

"Sheesh, sounds awful."

"And I'm not the only one who suffers this intolerable condition. About 3,000 macaques share my misery." Pointing at the free macaque's chest, he said, "You're one of the few lucky ones."

Acknowledging his freedom, the wild macaque nodded in agreement.

"Each year, we're stolen from our mamas, then subdued with chains and starvation until we obey and pick up the many nuances of public street performance. I never had aspirations to perform! But we're forced to dance while wearing doll-like face masks so that motorists give us a quick second glance, confusing us with diminutive humans."

"Twisted," said the wild macaque.

"Despite being a living distraction, I'm relieved to say I haven't caused a roadside accident yet."

"What's it all for?"

"All our painful efforts are intended to bring the humans a bowl full of rupiahs. I'm thankful for the sounds of a few coins dropping against the bottom of the clay bowl, because it means my owner is happy and I won't be starved that day." With downcast eyes, he looked over at his empty bowl.

"I wish I could help."

"Help? Help?" The macaque paced frantically. "The only way to help macaques trapped in horrendously dire conditions is to end the cruel animal trade and return us to the wild. I'd enjoy nothing more than making 15-foot leaps of freedom from tree to tree in the company of fellow macaques in our tropical forests."

"Dude, it's what I do all day," said the free macaque with a big smile.

"I was carefree too, before being chained up for life." The enslaved macaque turned his back and grumbled, "Now, if you'll excuse me, I've got a rusty unicycle and a whipping waiting for me."

ON ZOO ORANGUTANS

"Look at that one, with the red hair and goofy buck tooth smile." Buster, a bright-haired orangutan, pointed to the crowd of people outside his enclosure.

"Where, where?" asked Lou. The orangutan shuffled eagerly back and forth across the stone path, looking for the red haired spectacle.

"Ugh, he's gone. You missed him. Probably standing at the giraffe exhibit by now," said Buster.

"Ah, geez, what a bummer. The redheaded ones are rare." Lou plonked down on a flat rock as the crowd moved on. "I don't know why they come to see us."

Buster shook his furry orange head. "No, no, Lou,

you've got it all wrong. The people come to the zoo so that we can see *them*, point out their peculiarities, and have a blast. Zoo audiences serve as a form of entertainment. Whenever they show up, it's a time of social bonding for us red apes."

"You kind of develop a soft spot for the millions of humans who pay big bucks for zoo tickets just so that we can gawk at them." Lou sniffled and placed one paw over his heart.

"Yeah, up-close human encounters are an opportunity, and given their idiosyncrasies, these people will tug at your heartstrings," replied Buster.

Lou wiped his finger under his nose. "You almost want to help preserve their habitat just so they can keep visiting and entertaining us."

As the two orangutans waited for the next group of people to stop by, they chatted further.

"How's it going with Juniper?" asked Buster. "Is she attractive?"

"Ah, my dream date from the zoo across town. We met over the internet. I can't wait to see her again. I'd recognize her thoughtful eyes and wispy, extended goatee immediately." Lou scratched his head, looked around for his tablet, but instead picked up a banana. "You know, the zoo's got this new high-tech way of determining whether we'll hit it off before moving us in together." The orangutan peeled the banana and noshed on it leisurely.

"Yeah, internet dating is the latest fad for captive orangutans. There's an app, even for apes."

A new crowd of people showed up at the exhibit. Buster jumped up and down excitedly, pointed, and shouted to Lou again, "Look at that one, over there! The guy carrying a tablet in his messenger case, scratching his head, and eating a banana!"

"Where, where?"

ON OCELOT TRANSLOCATIONS

"Howdy! I haven't seen you before. Your scent is unfamiliar too. You're new around here, aren't you?" asked the Texas ocelot.

"Yep, I guess. Weird story." Glancing around the unfamiliar landscape, the ocelot started to explain. "See, I was having the time of my life in Sonora, Mexico. As a wildcat with a perfectly camouflaging coat of fur, I'd laze around on a comfy tree branch all day. It was like a perpetual siesta. At night, the tropical forests would teem with delicious frogs, fish, and iguanas for me to catch, tear up, and swallow whole." Salivating, the ocelot licked his lips.

"Hidden by the thick Mexican vegetation, I was safe from anacondas, pumas, and other predators that would otherwise make a meal out of me." The wildcat even shared the details of his romantic life in Mexico. "Juanita, a girlfriend who lived in one of the five territories over which I prowled, was about to make me a proud dad. I pictured teaching my young a bunch of tricks that wild ocelots perform, like only going out on cloudy days to preserve our stealth or clawing logs to mark our vast territories. My blue-eyed youngins would've learned the protocol from good old dad, so they'd make it in the forests of Mexico. *Por favor* and *gracias* went a long way there." The ocelot paused and smiled. "I had everything. In fact, I couldn't believe I had it so good."

"Yeah?" asked the Texas ocelot, inching closer as he listened intently. "Then what?"

"One day, as I minded my own business deep in the Mexican brush, my sharp ears picked up the sound of rubber truck tires coming to a screeching halt. A few huge, muscular guys dressed in camo got out, and suddenly I found myself sulking in a live trap. Then it all went dark."

The Texas wildcat's ears perked up. "Mm-hmm. Go on."

"Next thing I knew, I woke up somewhere in the brush of southern Texas."

"Good golly, what a story. I've heard up here, we ocelots are on the endangered species list. I suppose the government is trying to boost our populations by kidnapping Mexican ocelots and translocating them here to Texas, like they wouldn't notice the difference. It's no secret, except to unsuspecting Mexican ocelots, like you. By the way, they call me Jethro."

The Mexican ocelot replied, "And I'm Pedro."

"Well, Pedro, how do you like it here?"

"I don't know, Jethro. After being dramatically torn from my full, peaceful life in Mexico and reluctantly translocated to foreign brush, I'm still in a bewildering state of culture shock."

ON ZOO GIRAFFES

"I miss the good old days of free living," mumbled Ralph from his tiny indoor enclosure. For the 18-foot wild giraffe, Ralph's cell was nothing like what he was used to on the tropical grasslands of the dry savannas, and even worse, too bare and simplistic for his feistiness and social intelligence.

"Yep," replied Sammy, who shared the limiting space. "The wild home range was where it was at. You could roam for 500 square miles, tasting the freedom in the wind, feeling the warm sun on your chestnut-spotted fur, and getting your choice of acacia tree leaves and shoots to pick from. Even the thorns didn't stop us from foraging all day."

"I miss Nate, Annie, and the rest of the gang. All 20 of us had a fun time together, daring to go out to the edges of the savannas, staring down a lion half a mile away, and kicking at hungry hyenas." Ralph heaved a long sigh, one that stretched as long as his graceful six-foot neck.

"Yep, now we're horribly deprived of a good time." Sammy contorted his lips and grumbled. "Looking for a hot date is not even in the cards for us anymore."

"Bachelor parties are a thing of the past too."

Sammy indulged in a moment of reminiscence. "The whole crew would star gaze, get drunk off the berries of the marula trees, and sing our hearts out in the vastness of the African savanna on karaoke night."

"It was a blast." Ralph dreamily gazed into the freedom that lay beyond their enclosure.

"Now all we get to look forward to is ongoing stress, possibly being euthanized, accidentally getting our necks trapped in the zoo fence, or wearing a bulky transmitter on the top of our heads so that handlers can understand our habits."

"In general, a shorter life span awaits us."

"And humans have the nerve to celebrate World Giraffe Day." Sammy kicked the hay on the cement floor. "What a con."

ON ELEPHANT CONSERVATION

"Eleanor! Hurry up!" Elijah yelled with a youthful squeal.

"I'm coming," Eleanor replied, huffing and puffing as she clumsily ran forward to catch up with the herd of adult females, adult males, and a few lumbering young ones.

Finally, the juvenile elephant caught up.

"What took you so long? The herd is almost at the water hole," said Elijah.

"You won't believe what happened to me once those helicopter blades started whirring, and the herd ran off without me."

Elijah's long-lashed eyes grew wide. "What happened?" An animated conversation began.

"Humph. There I was, trailing at the end of the herd, minding my own business, not hurting even the cattle egrets sitting on my back and gobbling up parasites."

Elijah eagerly listened. "Uh-huh?" His tail whooshed at a hungry cattle egret.

"Out of the blue, from the helicopter overhead, I was shot with a tranquilizer dart right on the behind. Those researchers can brag about good aim. But then again, it's hard to miss an elephant's behind."

Elijah's floppy ears flapped in the breeze. "Then what?" he asked.

"I felt woozy from the effects of the synthetic opioid and collapsed. I could have suffocated under my own weight, if those researchers weren't careful! Little did I know they began to hastily collect blood samples, then intrusively collect fecal samples. They measured my tusk and neck, then entered the data on a laptop—all in the name of research!"

"Ugh, what in the world do they want the stinky mess for?"

"Probably to determine our gut health. The humans are disturbingly obsessed with our daily habits. Anyway, I eventually came to and managed to stand on my wobbly legs. When I regained my wits, I ran to the safety of the herd. The whole experience was unnerving."

Elijah let out a big sigh. "If anything."

"Humans certainly go about elephant conservation in the strangest of ways."

Elijah looked at Eleanor and pointed with his trunk. "What's that thing around your neck?"

Eleanor looked down. "Unbelievable!" Her trunk flew up in a rage. "Those dimwits bolted a tracker around me. Now I'm stuck wearing an annoying 22-pound piece of crap!"

The two elephants ambled, with Eleanor complaining nonstop. "Tranquilizers, 60-millimeter needles, blood samples, fecal samples, tape measures, and now this: a damn GPS satellite tracker. I feel like a frivolous science experiment instead of a majestic wild elephant." She launched her trunk high into the hot tropical air in defiance. "It's all supposedly in the name of elephant conservation. Look what our species has to endure to survive. And it's the so-called helpful humans who started all this encroachment of our habitat in the first place!"

ON BIRD BANDING

Two blue-footed boobies sat on top of a wavy, grooved rock jutting 100 feet out of the surface of the ocean in the Galápagos Islands.

"Now I may be known as a birdbrain, but it doesn't mean I like being caught, banded, and then set free like nothing happened. Now I have to wear this aggravating band around my ankle for the rest of my life." With a frown, Bodie looked down at his spectacularly blue-webbed feet.

A rushing wave thrashed against the glistening basalt rock, spraying the boobies with salt water.

"You too?" replied Bob. "Fortunately, I paired up with

Mable before I got banded. It's our instinct to mate for life, banded or not. I'm grateful she accepts me without complaint. But then again, not even infidelity could separate two boobies committed to each other forever. How 'bout you?"

"I'm not so lucky, being banded while single. It's ruining my dating life," Bodie complained. "We all know, the bluer my feet, the better the chances I have of scoring a mate. This bright-yellow band around my ankle disguises the healthy blueness of my feet, and reduces my chances for dating success to virtually nil. It eclipses my finest asset. I'm doomed to be a failed romantic, a loner, a cantankerous blue-footed booby for the rest of my life."

"Humans sure have a weird way of supposedly saving the species." Bob turned his head and nonchalantly gazed out over the untamed ocean.

Bodie said, "Even though we're just boobies, stupid by some standards, we know exactly what's going on." The booby stood up, dramatically slapped one blue foot on the rock, then did the same with his other foot.

"Humans think they're smart—studying our behavior, social structure, faithfulness between mates, reproduction rate, and lifespan—by clipping a bothersome band around our ankles," muttered Bob.

"Well, they should study my love life. They'll find it to be pathetic, because I don't have one," whined Bodie, inching his feathered body back down onto the rock. "And it's got nothing to do with personality. I've got a fantastic one." He flicked his tail sharply. "I say it's all because of the awful bird band."

"Here's to that."

Bodie wailed, "I thought I'd be a father at my age, proud of two little chicks who'd also boast of exceptionally blue feet, just like dear old dad. But noooo. The bird band prevents an attractive female booby from noticing my true-blue qualities and giving me the privilege of being a glowing father."

"Yep."

The blue-footed boobies calmy watched the fierce ocean tides roll, their feathers ruffling in the gusts of wind.

"The garish yellow band doesn't even match my feathers."

"How tacky."

ON WILD-ANIMAL CROSSING SIGNS

Two white-tailed deer chatted by the edge of the road next to the deer-crossing sign. Under their feet grew mushrooms and grasses, a banquet fit for midwestern deer.

"I'm really impressed with the humans," said Drew. "They put up all sorts of animal-crossing signs to protect our welfare. There are deer-crossing signs for us. There are llama-crossing signs for Buck and Alice in the desert. There are cow-crossing signs for Buttercup and the herd in the pastures down yonder. There's even a hedgehog-crossing sign so good ol' Pete can make it safely back to his burrow."

Daryl nibbled on a vine. "Yeah, I always tell my fawns to cross exactly at the crossing sign. That way, the humans will be expecting us. Anywhere else is taking pure chance. No way to justify risking that."

"I guess that's what the signs are for. I mean, with all these signs, the humans have got the whole animal kingdom covered. They're really looking out for us!"

Winston, a striking stag with a head full of antlers, ambled up. "Did you hear about Cheech?"

Drew asked, "No, what happened?"

"He got hit by a speeding jeep on Route 53."

"What? Didn't he follow the signs?" asked Drew.

"Guess not. He was always a careful one, though. So I'm not sure."

"Well, who's at fault?" asked Daryl, being the most practically minded of the three. "Someone's got to pay the price."

Winston answered straightforwardly, "I blame the humans."

"And the humans blame us for not following the animal-crossing signs," exclaimed Drew. "It's like they assume we don't take the time to read the pictures."

"Luckily, they can't sue wild animals," said Winston, exhaling with relief.

"Oh, you know the humans have considered it," huffed

Daryl, "especially the lawyers, looking at it from all angles before half-heartedly giving up. But it's still in the back of their minds, waiting for an opportunity."

"How's he doing?" asked Drew.

"Cheech is okay, limping, but okay."

"What about the human?"

"The human was grumbling for several minutes, throwing his hands up in the air, and pacing back and forth," replied Winston.

"Oh, because he felt bad to have injured Cheech?"

"No, because Cheech's hoof crushed his fender."

Daryl astutely observed, "Fortunately, the human didn't hit Buttercup or any of the other cows. Otherwise, he would've tried to sue the owner of the farm, the dairy corporation, and the government itself."

"What a litigious society."

"It's best to never get involved."

"Uh, yeah."

ON THE BLACK-NAPED PHEASANT-PIGEON

"You know, at one point in the recent past, they thought we didn't exist—disappeared like stardust from the time line of natural history," said Ethel from her nest in the rich soil under the ferns in the forests of Fergusson Island in Papua New Guinea.

"Well, we unfortunately managed to be spotted because of Dave. He walked right into the view of the motion-triggered camera trap," complained Mildred.

"It had to be Dave, of all black-naped pheasant-pigeons, didn't it? Now we'll be on the humans' radar forever." Ethel gave the soil an angry kick with her scrawny yellow pheasant-pigeon feet, scattering the dirt in all directions.

"They'll track us down, monitor our every move, relocate us to some horrible, unfamiliar island that I wouldn't call home in a million years, and, in other words, make our lives a living hell—all in efforts to conserve our critically endangered species." Mildred rapidly flicked her long, thick black tail.

Ethel, reminiscing about the golden days, boasted, "We managed to evade being documented by scientists since 1882."

"Over 100 peaceful years! All of a sudden, they discover we're not extinct. Drats!"

"The scientists were relentless, hiking up steep terrain, interviewing locals, camping out under the treetops in the treacherous forest, then finally finding us on the remotest part of the island 3,000 feet above sea level," Ethel hissed, as any irritated black-naped pheasant-pigeon would.

"Darn villagers gave us away," snapped Mildred.

"Don't forget good-old Dave. If it weren't for him, we'd still be on the down-low."

Mildred recalled the scene etched in her brain. "Once the scientists found us, they engaged in a whole 20 minutes of a bizarre series of masculine fist-bumping and hollering, as if they'd stumbled upon the legendary yeti or the infamous bigfoot."

"Or a fantastical winged unicorn, for goodness' sake."

Mildred bobbed her head in characteristic pheasant-pigeon fashion. "Hmm, I don't mind being likened to a unicorn. They're rather exquisite."

Ethel rolled her red eyes. "Yeah, you're right. The resemblance is uncanny."

ON THE ELEPHANT LIQUOR HEIST

Petey stomped through the South Asian jungle, his brother lumbering beside him. "The jungle's such a bore," complained Petey.

Ralph agreed without hesitation. "Meh."

Both elephants wandered aimlessly between the trees, with nothing to do and nowhere in particular to go. Then Petey lifted his trunk. "What's that smell?"

Ralph, too, sampled the air. "I don't know."

Petey, the younger, mischievous one, said, "Let's follow it."

They rushed onward, searching for excitement and the source of the intoxicating aroma. In the middle of a clearing, not far from where Petey and Ralph first picked up the smell, dozens of earthen pots sat on the jungle floor. Curious, Petey dipped his trunk into the liquid inside and tasted it. "Wow!"

Intrigued, Ralph drank from the pots too.

"What is this?" asked Petey. "I feel woozy, good, but woozy."

"I don't know, but it's so good that if Mom and Dad find out, they'll ground us for life."

Just then, the sounds of their parents' voices pierced the thick jungle air. "Petey! Ralph!"

"Oh no!"

The large juveniles hid futilely behind the slender trunk of the Indian butter tree. Their parents, along with two dozen relatives, arrived at the very spot where the earthen pots sat.

"Mmm." Mom plunged her trunk into the sweet-smelling liquid.

Dad followed her example. "A gift from the heavens!"

All 24 elephants in the herd arrived and drank joyfully from the pots, smashing them to pieces after emptying them.

"The tropical flower of the butter tree makes a sumptuous late-afternoon cocktail!" squealed Mom.

"The entire herd loves it!" Dad relished the liquor.

The massive herd finished off every drop of the pure *muhua*, the beverage made extra-tempting by its 45 percent alcohol content. The drunken elephants dozed. As they slumbered, forest officials ran to the scene where the mahua was left out to ferment and tried in vain to rouse the animals. Only after banging on drums did Petey, Ralph, Mom, Dad, and the rest of the herd wake up and flee.

"What was that?" asked Petey, after he'd found safety farther into the jungle.

Mom replied, "Pure mahua, Petey. Good find."

"That's my boy!" Dad added. "What an incredible buzz, despite coming from such tiny pots!"

"It must be because we don't metabolize liquor the same way humans can," explained Mom.

Dad raised his trunk triumphantly and hollered so loudly that his words echoed through the jungle. "The watering hole takes on a whole new meaning in the jungles of South Asia!"

And in the distance, the sour forest officials cleaned up from the elephant party.

ON LIFELONG CROW GRUDGES

"I'll never forget it. An entire three months of my life wasted in a two-foot-by-two-foot plexiglass enclosure at the nature center. I was ripped away from the whole family." Fritz perched on a tree limb overlooking a road winding around the forest preserve. "How I missed foraging at the garbage dumps with the flock all day and distracting river otters so we could swoop down, steal their fish, and make a clean getaway. Worked like a charm every time."

Spatz, perched on the same tree, picked up on Fritz's frustration. "Sounds lonesome. What did you do?"

"It was terrible. What could I do?" erupted Fritz.

"I sat idly on my perch for hours, watching all the impressionable nature center visitors watching me. I guess an American crow wasn't as entertaining as the slithering 54-inch western fox snake in the enclosure four feet down. Whatever, being held captive was mind-numbing if not frustrating beyond belief. It was like keeping an active seven-year-old in a cage and expecting him to be cool about it."

"How'd you escape?"

"I finagled my way out." Fritz shook his tail feathers in excitement. "Given my smarts and exceptional tool making skills, I finally did just that. I ripped off a three-inch splinter of wood from the perimeter of my cage and shimmied the lock. Presto! I was home free."

"Bravo, Fritz. You solidify our reputation as being among the most intelligent animals on the planet."

With a casual confidence, Fritz boasted, "On a certain level, I'd say even smarter than some humans."

"Fortunately, not all humans are alike, with most of them knowing wild crows need the open sky and the opportunity to roost in groups numbering in the hundreds."

"And we'll sound the call when they threaten our way of life!" Fritz exclaimed boldly and cawed proudly.

Spatz joined his friend in a series of loud caws.

Calming down, Fritz said nonchalantly, "But I'll never forget the bird keeper's expression when he saw the empty enclosure. In fact, I'll never forget the guy's face. Five years later, I still dive-bomb the moron who held me captive."

"Serves him right."

ON WORLD LEMUR DAY

"We have our own day!" squealed Buttons. The young lemur raised up her thin, furry gray arms in excitement.

"Big deal," replied Margo, an alpha female.

"No, you don't understand. As the world's oldest primates, we have a special day set aside every October to be recognized and adored. It's called World Lemur Day."

"It doesn't matter. We're still on the verge of extinction." Margo flicked her long ringed tail.

Buttons' fervor was unstoppable. "Having our own day is an event of mammoth proportions!"

"Oh, and just look what happened to the mammoths! They're extinct!"

"But the humans gave us a day!" Trying to make her point, the young lemur grew exasperated.

"Well, it's probably for selfish reasons. I mean, our species goes way back on the time line of the evolution of primates, making us ancient ancestors to humans. We're like odd cousins to them, so they're celebrating our genetic contributions to their evolution. Nothing special about humans celebrating a part of themselves."

"But—"

"Listen, if we get our own day, it's probably because the humans want to bring more attention to us."

"Exactly." Buttons, finally being heard, sat back in relief.

"But that goal backfires, because the more humans know about us, the more they want to keep us as pets. And you know how devastating it is to keep a wild primate as an exotic pet," warned Margo.

The inexperienced lemur crossed her arms.

"I mean, we've got complicated dietary needs. We don't exactly survive on pizza and ice cream. Vets don't even want to touch us because of the possibility of disease transmission. What happens when we get diabetes? Plus, as social animals, we need other lemurs, not humans. Do you remember Sally from North Carolina, where it's legal to own a lemur? Poor thing nearly lost her tail by chewing on it incessantly as a coping strategy for living in isolation from the family group!"

Grudgingly, Buttons listened.

"Do you want to become physically and psychologically maldeveloped? No lemur in her right mind wants that. No one can tame a wild lemur either, attractive as that sounds. We're not going to remain cute and cuddly toward humans forever. Mildred's owner didn't appreciate her attempts to show dominance by chasing, grabbing, and biting her. The terrified lady hid from her in the bathroom with the door closed and called emergency responders, frantically asking them what to do!"

Buttons slid down her seat and sighed.

"In the end, owners of pet lemurs don't want us anymore. And where are they going to send us? To the lemur orphanage? Come on, World Lemur Day is just another day, dressed up in bells and whistles and signifying nothing."

Buttons was diminished to a whisper. "But it's our . . . day."

ON MIAMI'S WILD MACAWS

"Mama, what happened on the night that all the macaws in Miami talk about?" asked Vic.

Mama Vivian, a vibrant blue-and-yellow macaw, replied to her fledgling, "Oh, dearie, it was a heck of a night, one that saved us wild macaws from the poachers."

"What's a poacher?" asked the one-year-old fledgling.

"A poacher is someone who hunts or catches wild animals," Mama Vivian replied. "In Miami, unfortunately, it's legal to poach wild macaws, because we're not a native species. The poachers shoot us with net guns to catch us, breaking our legs and wings in the process. Then they trade us in the multibillion-dollar exotic pet trade, broken legs and all."

"Oh." Vic's eyes drooped.

"There, there, darling. Although there's currently no state law to protect wild macaws from the poachers, we've devised our own strategies to keep our flocks safe from the illegal pet trade."

Vic's eyes lit up. "Really?"

"Get comfy, son, as I'm about to tell you a story that changed the life of Miami macaws."

The baby macaw snuggled closer to his mama in their nest inside the hole of a tree.

"Now, it was known to us local macaws that a pair of poachers by the names of Rob and Hector terrorized us. In fact, Aunt Tillie had a fledgling, whom the poachers snatched right from her treetop nest in the middle of the night. She fought hard to chase them off, but with no luck."

"Then what happened?"

"The next year, Aunt Tillie had another fledgling, your cousin Sky. This time, she was prepared. The night Rob started climbing the ladder up to the nest to steal her fledgling, Aunt Tillie put her plan into action. She flew down, temporarily leaving Sky vulnerable. See, when you're a macaw, you use what you've got. And macaws have the ability to mimic human vocalizations."

"Uh-huh?" The fledgling listened wide-eyed.

"As soon as Aunt Tillie flew to the ground below, she started talking—in Hector's voice."

"What did she say?"

"I'm getting to it. Be patient. Now, it was nightfall and dark. As Rob climbed, Aunt Tillie said, 'Hey, Rob!' Working alone that night, the poacher was stunned. He called out, 'Hector? Is that you? Where are you?'"

Vic chuckled.

"Then the battle began. Aunt Tillie, still mimicking Hector's voice, said, 'I've got news for you, Rob. You're a slob.' The poacher whipped his head around. 'What? Shut up, Hector.' Then Aunt Tillie turned on the heat. 'You're not only a slob, you're stupid. And I slept with your wife!'"

The fledgling bowled over laughing.

Mama Vivian continued her tale. "Rob turned red in the face and yelled. 'Don't you dare!' He jumped off the ladder and started chasing no one deep into the night.' Aunt Tillie flew up to her nest to find Sky asleep peacefully, not one feather disturbed."

"All right!" Vic cheered.

"The next thing we heard through the macaw grapevine was that Rob gave up poaching, saying it drove him crazy."

That night, Mama Vivian and Vic fell asleep in the treetops without a care in the world.

ON SEA TURTLES AND PLASTIC BAGS

Ned paddled his large, angular green flippers through the sapphire blue waters of the Pacific Ocean. "It's getting harder and harder to differentiate between a juicy planktonic marine member of the Scyphozoa class and a Slim's grocery bag."

"Yep, jellyfish are either getting smarter at evading us, or we're losing our touch." Kyle calmly swam through the water alongside his buddy of 20 years.

"I don't know," replied Ned. "Jellyfish and plastic bags are nearly identical, with thin, transparent skin and the nimble ability to propel through the water. Plus, neither has a brain."

"How'd they survive so long without one?" asked Kyle, observing his surroundings for dangers.

"Oh, I wouldn't underestimate jellyfish," Ned answered. "I wouldn't underestimate plastic bags either. Thousands of the smartest sea turtles with the strongest sense of self-preservation are horribly tricked every year into eating plastic bags pulsing along the ocean currents like jellyfish."

The beginnings of a floating island of oceanic garbage, triple the size of France, loomed ahead. Kyle warned, "Watch out, we're swimming straight toward the slow-spiraling water of the Great Pacific Garbage Patch."

"You know a garbage pile is massive when it's recognized by its own name." Ned observed with the coolness of a wise sea turtle. "There'll soon be literally more plastic in the oceans than fish."

Rather than risk becoming perilously trapped in the litter, the turtles swerved and redirected their course.

"All it takes is one plastic bag, and *boom*, it's a death sentence."

"Yep, it happened to Karim," agreed Kyle. "Poor guy. He mistook a deadly plastic bag for a delicious *Aurelia aurita*, familiarly known as the moon jelly. He skillfully protected himself from the sting of jellyfish tentacles, but he had another thing coming when munching on a plastic bag. The bag lodged in Karim's digestive tract, and he was done for, never to be seen alive in the Pacific again."

Ned and Kyle swam steadily.

Kyle broke the silence. "They say some jellyfish are immortal, specifically the *Turritopsis dohrnii* species, destined to live forever."

"They also say plastic bags are immortal," Ned griped, "specifically the single-use grocery bag species, destined to pollute our oceans forever."

And the sea turtles dived, disappearing 900 feet into the ocean depths.

ON CHAINED ELEPHANTS

Two young elephants chatted inside the elephant sanctuary. Their eyes lit up as they freely roamed over the green grasses and beneath the towering trees. With contagious smiles and loud trumpeting, they sounded the joys of freedom.

"Life was different before I came to the sanctuary," bragged Onisha. "My Sri Lankan captors loved me so much that they kept me on chains all day, letting me roam free at night while secured to a 145-foot metal chain." Onisha dug into the ground for a root. She popped a tasty one into her mouth. "They were quite generous and protective, saying it was to prevent me from wandering into neighboring farmers' fields and being wounded, getting killed for ivory, or injuring other elephants and visitors." She glanced at her companion. "In fact, they loved me so much that they put up a website claiming to conserve elephants, explaining my captive situation to unwitting visitors convincingly."

A playfully competitive elephant, Ditya attempted to outdo her new friend. "Well, my captors at the Nepali zoo kept me on chains 19 hours a day, rendering me immobile, with one front foot and one back foot fastened to a cement block. I could barely move." She managed a weak smile. "However, I was valued so much that the zookeepers demanded I give one-hour rides to trekkers to help promote the country's tourism industry. I was lovingly struck with bullhooks that caused the scars I still have today." She lifted her trunk and pointed to the deep pink indentations numbering in the hundreds all over her body.

Orraya, an exquisite and matronly elephant, plucked delicious pieces of bamboo nearby. Upon picking up their conversation with her floppy ears, she sauntered up to the duo. "The greatest love of all is being shown to my older sister, Anong, who remains imprisoned in a Thailand zoo. During her 23 years of living in chains, the calves she lovingly bore were ripped from her, leaving her maternal heart empty."

Orraya's long-lashed eyes grew downcast. "I've known Anong to be remarkably social, but her forced isolation contributes to her fits of anger. The zookeepers respond by worsening her confinement, leaving her to stare forlornly into the dirty corner of her darkened cement enclosure. She has no regular access to drinking water, and she stands in her own filth."

The elephant paused for several minutes to control her hysteria. "After a lifetime of being shackled in metal chains to the cement floor and being whipped into submission, Anong no longer tries to break free. Her natural elephant behaviors have been offhandedly destroyed by the most-loving-of-all zoo handlers."

The two young elephants intertwined their trunks with the older one's.

Her eyes closed, Orraya whispered, "An elephant never forgets."

All three elephants, remembering the immense love showered upon them by their captors, buckled at the knees, dropped to the ground, and wept.

ON THE CAPTIVE ROBIN

"Look at Harry, pathetic," muttered Louie, an American robin perched on the cherry tree branch outside the nature center.

"Yep, being imprisoned in a two-foot-by-two-foot plastic enclosure with random holes for breathing is never a good thing for a wild songbird. Sadly, he doesn't even sing anymore." Jerry, also an American robin, sat on the branch too, gazing through the nature center window at their captive friend.

"I don't know what he does all day," Louie wondered out loud. "A songbird needs constant stimulation from the great outdoors, the feel of the soft grass as we hop on it, the warmth of the sun's rays on our feathers, the drops of rain, the chance to gobble up scrambling insects, and the joys of getting tipsy on fermented berries in springtime. We were born to fly in the vast blue sky. In his plastic cell, Harry can't even get off the ground." Louie observed, "When a visitor playfully pokes her finger through the hole in the sparse enclosure, Harry pecks at it, believing it's a worm. He's going completely berserk in there."

"Yep, it's unnatural and horrific." Then Jerry recalled, with admiration, "Back in the day, Harry was the man, the greatest Casanova that ever lived, pairing up with a fine new female every spring. The females adored him and his stunning courtship displays. He'd belt rich, soulful melodies, give his wings a shake, fluff out his tail feathers, and puff out his throat like there was no tomorrow. And the ladies loved it."

"Now look at him, held in solitary confinement in a plastic enclosure for humans' viewing pleasure."

"Puzzling." Jerry shook his head, baffled. "It's not like the American robin is a rare bird or on the brink of extinction. There's 310 million of us. We're the most familiar and widespread songbird in the nation. Everyone has seen a robin in the fields, forests, parks, or their backyard, whether they're on the East Coast or West Coast or even in Alaska. Why catch one and put him up for exhibition like he's some prehistoric dinosaur?"

Genuinely confused, Louie quibbled, "I don't get it either. Humans proudly make us the official bird in three states, Connecticut, Michigan, and Wisconsin, consider us iconic, then unnecessarily imprison poor Harry. Humans are something else."

"Contradictory, if anything," muttered Jerry.

Looking through the window, Louie produced a sharp whinny, a robin's warning call. "Seeing our friend in his deplorable condition, set up by the humans, I'm compelled to ask: Who's the real birdbrain here?"

ON SEAHORSE LOVE

Liam, a long-snouted seahorse, slowly propelled himself forward with his dorsal fins in the calm coastal waters. "I don't know why we don't get the conveniences of online dating down here in the ocean."

"Meh, it's probably because dating apps aren't waterproof." Elijah, a six-inch spotted long-snouted seahorse, casually anchored himself to seaweed with his curly tail.

"It's so hard to find a soulmate. I mean, we're not the best of swimmers, and noticing a potential mate is almost next to impossible because we keep ourselves camouflaged."

"Well, don't feel so bad, Liam. Given the loss of our habitat and the risk of tumbling into fishermen's bycatch, falling in love can be fatal."

"That's a harsh thing to say, Elijah. I'd rather feel true love for a short amount of time rather than feel lonesome for the rest of my life."

"Uh, like I said. Love can be the end of it all."

"What do you mean?"

"Remember Aiden?" Elijah began slowly. "He was a charismatic big-bellied seahorse, an entire foot long, with bright-yellow color and a charming Australian accent. He fell in love once. That's all it took. He stumbled upon a lovely seahorse named Bea. The companions shared an incredible romance, greeting each other in the mornings with flirtatious pirouettes, just to make sure the other was alive and well. Their daily dances strengthened their lifelong bond, and even synchronized their reproductive cycles."

"Sounds blissful." Liam gazed off dreamily.

"Oh, I wouldn't talk so fast," cautioned Elijah. "One day, Bea wrapped her tail around some vegetation. The next thing she knew, she was caught as bycatch by trawl fishing, hoisted onto a boat, and sold for pittances so that she could be dried and made into a souvenir or be used in traditional medicine." Even wise Elijah appeared stunned by the reality of the 70 million seahorses who suffer the same fate every year.

"That's dreadful." With a flap of his fins, Liam asked, "What happened to Aiden?"

Elijah let go of the seaweed growing in the shallow water and propelled himself upward. "Aiden was pregnant with their fry. The next morning, when he looked for Bea to perform their daily dance, she wasn't there. He desperately searched the mangroves, coral reefs, seagrass beds, and estuaries—places she could have wandered into—but without luck. Finally, he heard that the fishermen had been there."

Liam popped his eyes open in shock. "Oh gosh."

"Aiden felt so heartbroken that he refused to eat, not even the tastiest of zooplankton or crustaceans. When he felt muscular contractions, he gave birth to their fry, but no longer felt the drive to reproduce ever again. His immunological function declined." With a sniffle, Elijah finished the tale. "Long story short, Aiden felt extreme emotional and physiological distress upon being separated from the mate he loved so dearly. Not too long after her disappearance, Aiden, lonely and saddened, perished, some say of a broken heart."

"What a nightmare."

"In today's oceans, love hurts for wild seahorses."

ON ALBATROSSES AND PLASTICS

Diane and Angel, two southern royal albatrosses with wingspans stretching 11 feet, soared above the ocean for a continuous 1,000 miles, resting on the water briefly when the wind stilled, but never once touching land.

"We've trusted the ocean for 50 million years to give us food," said Diane, with a hint of melancholy. "We simply made shallow dives and scooped up the fish, plankton, and carrion floating on the surface."

"Yep, now there's an ominous new addition to what's floating on the ocean's surface," said Angel, with a full-body shiver.

"Plastic. Ugh." Diane dived down, then soared up. "It's killing our young."

"The strong stomachs of adult albatrosses vomit the plastics, but the fragile stomachs of our chicks are cut by the sharp pieces we accidentally feed them. All it takes is two ounces of plastic." A tear formed in Angel's eyes. "Then, sadly, they're gone."

"I've flown over too many carcasses of young albatrosses leaving plastic bottle caps, plastic cigarette lighters, and plastic shards in their feathery remains. What a tragedy. The plastic endures longer than their bones."

Confounded, Angel said, "I don't know how Wisdom, the oldest known living wild bird, manages to survive 70 years and counting on Midway Atoll, the Hawaiian archipelago where the largest colony of albatrosses nest. Being the hot mama she is, Wisdom continues at her ripe age to raise healthy little Laysan albatrosses."

"Yep, she's managed to avoid eating plastics. It's like she's got extraordinary senses." Diane flew in a straight course.

"But for the rest of us, if it looks like food, if it smells like food, then it must be food. Right?" asked Angel. "How deadly wrong we are!"

Without a single flap of her wing, Diane agreed.

"Yes, it's like going to the seafood counter at the neighborhood grocery and ordering a pound of shellfish. But instead of the shellfish, the seafood guy hands you a bag full of the plastic price tag thingies." She miraculously gained airspeed. "Only once you've swallowed the contents and lovingly regurgitated it into the bill of your chick do you realize it was nothing other than a death trap intent on killing what you hold most dear."

"No kidding. We're surrounded by all-you-can-eat plastic buffets. Hungry as we are, those floating red, green, and yellow bottle caps are going nowhere, except into the bellies of unsuspecting albatrosses or other innocent marine life." Angel glided in a half circle. "Plastic is appetizing to look at, being colorful. Plastic is delicious to smell, giving off an aroma similar to masses of tasty plankton. But it's nonetheless deadly to eat. What a twist of fate for hungry albatrosses scouring the ocean for a decent meal."

"Soon, the only place albatrosses will continue to enjoy life is in ancient maritime lore." And the beautiful albatrosses soared, catching and riding alternating layers of high- and low-pressure winds.

ON TROPHY HUNTING

Spencer, a magnificent South African zebra with a thick black-and-white mohawk, said, "I looked through the window of the lodge I happened to pass by and saw Jazz splayed out on the hardwood floor. I whispered, 'Psst! Jazz, what're you doin' down there?' He didn't bat an eyelash. Next thing I know, the pet dog casually walks all over him. I couldn't believe my eyes and bolted."

Colin, also a stunning zebra with a zigzag coat, replied, "Yeah, I've passed by that lodge too. Looking through the window in the next room, I saw Bartholomew, Rachel, Manchester, Dimitri, and Samantha, staring blankly ahead with their heads jutting out of gleaming wooden plaques on the wall. They looked like I'd just seen them yesterday, not a day older. After that, I ran for my life."

"What in the world was that all about?"

"It's called trophy hunting. Hunters kill us for sport," answered Colin, pulling back his ears as he stood on the grass in the middle of the savanna woodlands.

Confused, Spencer asked, "Sport? Isn't a sport between willing and equal competitors?" He paused, then asked, "And isn't a sport intended to bring enjoyment to participants?"

"Sure is."

"So how is a hunter wielding an automatic weapon against a defenseless zebra considered fair?" asked young Spencer. "Being shot with a rifle or crossbow while I'm peacefully grazing on the mixed grasslands in the Limpopo province isn't my idea of a good time." His ears strained forward.

"The enjoyment is definitely not mutual."

"Plus, there's no referees to call out foul play, no penalties, no rules of the game." Spencer grew exasperated. "How is trophy hunting a true sport?"

"I think the humans just pretty up their language to make their brutality appear civil," Colin answered, eyeing the next patch of grass to graze upon. "They even pay good money to kill us."

"Hunters shell out thousands of dollars to terrorize us?" shrieked Spencer. "Now we're involved in pay-to-play?"

"Not only that, but humans make hunting attractive by combining it with 10-day safaris, enforcing zero seasonal restrictions, conveniently picking hunters up from the airport, throwing in beer and wine, and, worst of all—guaranteeing mature zebras for the hunt, like dear ol' Jazz."

"Poor Jazz." Spencer sighed. "He was a handsome zebra stud. Now he's just a gorgeous rug."

"Then the hunters pose for pictures with us in our final moments. It's a bit surreal, seeing them resting their weapon of choice against our fallen, bloodied bodies while smiling ear to ear, as if they'd just performed a random act of kindness."

"Sheesh, humans and their ideas of fun sure are peculiar."

ON CAPTIVE ORCAS

Mimi and Ralph zoomed through the rushing blue waters of the ocean. The orcas rejoiced in their freedom, swimming their usual 40 miles each day. In the middle of their swim, Mimi said to Ralph, "Did you hear about Hugh?"

At 32-feet in length, Ralph was a gigantic killer whale. Despite having an intimidating size and the reputation for being one of the most fearsome predators in the ocean, he shook his head tenderly. "Yeah. What a tragedy."

"Poor guy didn't have a chance, being plucked from the ocean at age three, then isolated inside a teensy enclosure for years." Mimi's eyelids drooped in sadness.

"Yeah, the loneliness sure did a number on him." The friendly orcas sped through the ocean, diving to depths of 500 feet.

Mimi opened her mouth wide to capture a school of fish. "Even introducing a frisky romantic partner couldn't reverse the damage," she said after swallowing. "A whale bowl, they called it."

"Huh?"

"That's where they kept him, a massive wild orca in a bowl."

"And I thought goldfish were meant to be in bowls."

Ralph also opened his jaw to catch fish. "An orca bored and stressed beyond belief, forced to perform unnatural tricks for the sake of human entertainment. He'd either escape captivity or die trying. I don't blame him for banging his head against the concrete wall until, *poof*, he was out of his miserable condition."

Mimi glanced over at Ralph. "Had he been out here in the great expanse of the ocean with us, where he belonged, he'd still be around, you know, living to 80, like Gramps, instead of 15."

As the six-ton orcas navigated through the unending freedom of the sea, Ralph muttered with disappointment, "And humans think they have the highest IQ on the planet."

ON FOXHUNTING

"Okay, I'm glad there's a law here in the States to protect foxes from being killed by the hounds," said Ralph, a red fox with a gorgeous tail tipped in white, as he sat in the tilled fields.

"Yeah, but the hunters scare the living daylights out of us—for pure enjoyment." Max relaxed in the fields in his brother's company, keeping warm by wrapping his bushy tail around his nose.

"Right," agreed Ralph, as the autumn foliage gently fell. "But it's not so bad nowadays in comparison to decades prior when the hounds had leeway to rip us to shreds and the hunters would hand out our tails as trophies. I remember Gramps, before he was killed in his final foxhunt in his native Wales, bragging about how he had the wits to escape 20 matched pairs of hounds and elegantly dressed men on horseback countless times."

Max snickered. "They were dressed to kill."

"He said the excitement began with the shout of '*Tally-ho!*' and the hounds were off on the chase through the fields where they figured he was hiding. All Gramps could see through the tree branches were flashes of the bright scarlet coats and the crisp white pants worn by the huntsmen."

"He leaped six feet off the ground as he sped 30 miles per hour through the fields," Max recalled proudly.

"As he got older, Gramps would complain in his thick Welsh accent how dismally unfair it was that dozens of angry hounds with 300 million scent receptors on each of their noses and fierce men on swiftly galloping horses would chase a crafty 40-inch fox weighing a measly 10 pounds."

"Uh, being crafty is what saves our tails," Max pointed out.

Ralph sat in a moment of contemplation. "You know, it's like massive Canada raging an outright war with tiny Monaco for the sake of a good time."

"Or like a pride of hungry lions slapping around a scared titmouse for play," added Max.

Rolling back on the grass, Ralph chuckled. "Gramps would laugh hysterically every time he left the whole gang of hunters scratching their heads under their bowler hats and the hounds stumped and stopped in their tracks."

"Here in the States, they switched the rules and hunt coyotes instead," said Max. "Supposedly, they're bigger, faster, and stronger than us, making the thrill of the chase double the fun."

"Oh, so now they're just running an entirely different animal to exhaustion," protested Ralph. "It certainly improves matters for the whole animal kingdom."

And the two red foxes continued lazing under the red-orange Wisconsin sun.

ON ZONKEYS AND ZORSES

"Eh, mate, you look rather odd, like a short, stocky donkey with a wild zebra's black-and-white-striped legs," said a donkey wandering the open woodlands of Africa. "Kind of like a donkey on top and a zebra on the bottom."

"Er, I'm a zonkey. My pop's a zebra, and my ma's a donkey," said the zonkey.

"Oh, that explains it," replied the donkey. "So you're not a zedonk, with a donkey for a pop and a zebra for a ma."

"No, not a zedonk, just a zonkey."

"OK, got it, a zonkey. Maybe a zebrass or a zenkey?"

"I prefer zonkey."

"OK."

The African grasses grew tall but appeared shorter in the areas immediately surrounding the zonkey, as he continuously grazed on the tender green vegetation.

"You know, while passing through the African grasslands, I came across a zorse," said the donkey. "His pop's a zebra and his ma's a horse. He looks exactly like a horse but with zebra stripes."

"Yep, a zorse," agreed the zonkey, still contentedly grazing on herbs.

Theorizing out loud, the donkey uttered, "I don't think the zorse would exist without humans intervening. I mean zebras are found here in Africa, and wild horses are native to Europe and Asia."

"Right."

"Unfortunately, instead of grazing all day on the vast savanna, the zorse is put to work. The humans crossbreed the zorses and force them to carry people and things up and down mountains. His brother is not a trekking animal but is instead worse off, being forced to entertain humans in zoos due to his peculiar appearance." The donkey whipped his tail under the beating rays of the hot summer sun.

"I pull heavy loads too," said the zonkey with a

hopeless sigh. "Humans have discovered I have unusual stamina from my donkey side and amazing speed and strength from my zebra side."

The donkey said, "What a day it will be for the donkeys and the zonkeys and the zorses of the continent when the humans pull their own weight."

"Yep."

And the donkey joined the zonkey in grazing in the quiet woodland.

ON EXPERIMENTAL LAB BEAGLES

Sophie and Esmerelda, two French poodles, sat on the velvet couch, soaking in the rays of the sun and looking picture-perfect with their trimmed, polished nails, plush coats, and pink collars glistening with diamonds. "Look at the new foster, cowering in her cage. She never comes out," criticized Sophie.

"I hear Petunia has a tattoo on the inside flap of her ear," whispered Esmerelda.

"Ugh, a tattoo." Sophie shivered. "She's one of *those*."

Gretchen, an English bulldog, walked up to the poodles and said, "Don't you two spoiled princesses have a compassionate bone in your body?"

The French poodles whipped their heads to the right to see who was speaking to them in the rudest manner. "Excuse you?" barked Sophie.

"That tattoo was not her choice. Petunia spent her days in agony in an experimental lab before being rescued. The lab researchers gave her that ink. And the tattoo is not a form of self-expression. It's a series of letters that ID her," explained Gretchen. "No animal is eager to get inked. It's unnatural."

"Well," huffed Esmerelda.

"Petunia cowers in the corner of her cage because she's afraid of the world around her," the bulldog pointed out. "She grew up in severely inhumane conditions, spending her earlier life locked in a cold metal cage, never feeling the touch of grass or the warmth of the sun, like you two ladies have enjoyed all along."

"Well, I'll be," retorted Sophie, who spun her head around to look away from Gretchen.

"Her daily food was placed just outside her cage so she could be cruelly tempted by its smell, yet not taste it. Her teeth are rotted, and she nearly lost her life to euthanasia when a researcher determined she was becoming underweight. And it was no inconvenience, since the beagle incinerator was right inside the lab."

Esmerelda's eyes popped.

"Listen, beagles are the sweetest of dogs, a temperament that ironically makes them suitable for all sorts of awful animal testing. Ever seen a beagle rip a human to pieces? No, and that's why the researchers feel they can run painful experiments on them, using them in cosmetics testing or trying to develop treatments for human diseases, like diabetes and heart disease."

Sophie pursed her lips, containing her abomination.

"Well, at least Sophie and I are worth a pretty penny," boasted Esmerelda with a twist of her nose.

Gretchen didn't back down. "Petunia's life is more valuable than the $1,000 she was bought for by the lab. The horrific, global animal-testing market is worth over $10 billion."

The bulldog looked tenderly across the room at Petunia, who had made herself as small as possible in her cage. Then Gretchen returned her gaze to the poodles. "As a result of being experimented on in the lab, post-traumatic stress disorder got the best of her. Petunia shirks back at loud noises and sudden movements. She's traumatized. Being the ongoing subject of atrocious lab experiments and living in vile conditions will do that to anyone."

Sophie and Esmerelda sat with tightened facial expressions. Finally, Sophie burst out, "Come on

Esmerelda, we've got more pleasant things to do than listen to this drivel." With her nose up in the air, she led her sidekick out of the room.

Gretchen watched as the proud poodles left, then walked over to Petunia and lay down next to her.

ON ARIZONA'S WILD HORSES

Finney whinnied with pride. "We're an American treasure." The wilderness offered the black stallion wide-open spaces to enjoy uninterrupted grazing.

"Yep. We symbolize the freedom of the West like no other wild four-legged animal on earth," agreed Nellie, a brown stallion who leisurely nipped at the wide variety of weeds and shrubs. "A hundred strong gallop free into the Arizona sunset, leaving clouds of dust swirling in our wake."

"But, of course, there are always problems."

"Yep. Specifically, two-legged ones."

"The land can only support so many horses, around

a hundred of us in any given wild-horse territory." Finney's eyes widened, as he ground his teeth. "But they say that since large numbers of us graze down stretches of land, cattle ranchers no longer have enough food for all their animals."

"Some of the unruly ones get enraged, and local folks say it could be why so many of us, from adventurous stallions to loving mares, have been mysteriously shot dead." Nellie stopped chewing to ponder their stark new reality of the past few years.

"No one knows for sure the motive behind the killings or who's responsible. But one thing's clear: dead horses don't talk."

"Well, alive ones don't either, but that's a different story. Plus, it's not like those who live to tell the tale can nonverbally describe the bad guy, unless it's to someone as sympathetic as the horse whisperer."

"And how are we going to get the horse whisperer to come out here to the arid Arizona wilderness?" Finney asked in earnest.

Nellie answered by kicking the dirt.

The horses' ears picked up the whistling sound of the breeze through the trees.

Finney gazed into the infinite vastness of the wild-horse territory. "I remember with fondness the legendary stories of Wild Horse Annie, who fiercely protected us when our numbers dwindled."

"She was a two-legged hero, one of the good guys."

"Gals."

"Right."

"Now our populations are up and booming. Conflicts are bound to arise when different species share land," Finney reasoned with the wisdom of a horse who'd seen the wayward ways of the world. "The government tries to adopt us out to good homes, but some buyers' intents are questionable."

"A mutually well-regarded solution isn't merely a gallop away." Nellie's nostrils relaxed. "Whatever the case may be, you can take a wild horse out of the West, but you can't take the West out of a wild horse. We're as much a part of the West as cowboys and horseshoes—neither of which would exist without us anyway."

"We're here to stay."

"Amen."

ON MOUNTAIN GORILLAS AND ECOTOURISM

"I don't know why they don't screen tourists for the common cold before they unleash them upon us," complained Joe, a mountain gorilla living in Bwindi, a bustling national park in Uganda filled with wild residents, from bushpigs and colobus monkeys to antelopes.

"Definitely defeats the purpose of responsible ecotourism," mumbled George. He leaned back against the lush green bushes in the famed destination, a comfortable four feet from Joe.

"I mean, they pay big bucks, in the neighborhood of $800, to spend an hour sitting with us, watching us eat, play, and groom each other." Joe picked the juicy green leaves surrounding him and placed them between his lips. "All it takes is one sneeze from a sick human to disperse the contagious common cold virus into our vicinity."

"It's more like paying $800 to sentence us to our deaths."

"Yeah," agreed Joe. "We share 98 percent of DNA with humans. But that little 2 percent makes a huge difference. While the humans easily recover from the common cold, for us, coming down with the infectious disease is potentially fatal." The gorilla's thoughtful expression turned to one of sadness.

George paused in contemplation, then recollected an instance that occurred two weeks prior. "Jacob, the intimidating silverback, was so fed up after he and Polka lost their infant due to a respiratory disease caught from the humans that he began signing to the tourists to put on a mask or get out."

"How did that go?"

"Well, in response to his clear hand signals, the humans excitedly pointed at him, erupted in boisterous laughter, took a flurry of pictures, and continued coughing in his direction." Shaking his head, George remarked, "It's like they're not really that much smarter than us."

"I can't believe we share DNA with them."

"Ugh, me neither."

Thank you for reading *In Defense of Animalhood*.
If you enjoyed this romp with wildlife,
please consider leaving a review at your
favorite retailer, and help others discover books of
animal life and humor.

Books in the In Defense Of series
In Defense of the Grim Reaper
In Defense of Seniorhood
In Defense of Misfortune
In Defense of the Eighties
In Defense of Cupid

Visit my author website
www.riyapresents.com

CPSIA information can be obtained
at www.ICGtesting.com
Printed in the USA
LVHW050700140523
746941LV00001B/45